KIDS IN CRISIS

KIDS & DRUGS

Cynthia DiLaura Devore, M.D.

DEDICATION

To Carl, Michael, and Adam, for your patience.

Published by Abdo & Daughters, 4940 Viking Drive, Suite 622, Edina, Minnesota 55435.

Library bound edition distributed by Rockbottom Books, Pentagon Tower, P.O. Box 36036, Minneapolis, Minnesota 55435.

Printed in the United States.

Cover Photo credit: Bettmann
Interior Photo credits: Sygma, pages 5, 19, 21
　　　　　　　　　　　Woodfin Camp, pages 17, 23, 32
　　　　　　　　　　　Archive, page 27

Edited By Rosemary Wallner

Devore, Cynthia DiLaura, 1947-
　　　Kids and Drugs / by Cynthia DiLaura Devore.
　　　　　　　p.　　　cm. -- (Kids in Crisis)
　　　Includes bibliographical references and index.
　　　ISBN 1-56239-322-7
　　　1. Children -- United States--Drug use--Juvenile literature.
　　　2. Drug abuse--United States--Prevention--Juvenile literature.
　　　[1. Drug abuse.]　　　I. Title.　　　II. Series.
　　　HV5824.C45D4　　　1994
　　　362.29'17'083--dc20　　　　　　　　　　　　　　94-17687
　　　　　　　　　　　　　　　　　　　　　　　　　　　　　CIP
　　　　　　　　　　　　　　　　　　　　　　　　　　　　　AC

CONTENTS

1

NOTE TO PARENTS AND TEACHERS

Parents and teachers have an extraordinary task. They must try to nurture and guide children to become productive, happy adults in a world full of increasing dangers. Drugs and guns are widespread. Violence is glamorized on television and is rampant in the streets. Values are distorted. These are difficult times to be a child. These are also difficult times to be a parent or teacher.

This series is intended to help us keep our children safe in the midst of all this turmoil. The stories and exercises can accomplish this in part by helping young adults to develop their own skills at making thoughtful, critical decisions. Each book in the Kids in Crisis series begins with a story (based on a true incident) that illustrates each problem. The story presents children in grades five through seven with a reality-based approach to each topic.

The narrative is also meant to be instructional. The course of decision-making is mapped out as the story unfolds in a step-wise cumulative fashion building on the choices made by the children in the stories.

Today, children are experimenting with various types of drugs. The photo above shows children in Bangkok, Thailand, sniffing glue, while this young boy puffs on a cigarette.

In *Kids and Drugs,* the profile story is about a teenager hoping to improve his chances for a college football scholarship by taking anabolic steroids. The story provides readers with a slightly different look at the world of drugs. The intent is to dispel the notions that the only kids who use drugs are troubled kids, and the only drugs students need to be concerned about are hard drugs like crack cocaine. The escalation of the teenager's involvement is an accurate scenario of the progressive steps to drug use.

The next chapter discusses choices and consequences, with references back to the profile story. This provides an opportunity to discuss alternative choices. It also introduces the concept of impulsive versus thoughtful actions and accountability for choices.

The third chapter presents facts and statistics about drugs in a nonjudgmental fashion. This allows the reader to become better informed and thereby better able to develop critical thinking skills.

The next two chapters present the case for and against the legalization of drugs. Again, facts are presented so that students are encouraged to draw their own conclusions.

The sixth chapter returns to the profile story with a look at values that emerged as the incident unfolded.

Finally in "Your Turn," students complete projects or discuss issues they have garnered from the book.

Each book in this series should serve as a springboard for discussion between young people and their grown-ups. Ultimately, the more we communicate with our children at any level, the better equipped they will be to handle life's difficult choices when we may not be around to help them.

Your thoughts and comments on this topic or ideas for future topics are most welcome. The author, like you, is dedicated to the well-being of our children. Please address your comments to the author in care of the publisher.

2

PETER'S STORY

The following is based on a true story of a 17-year-old American high school student.

It was the spring of Peter's junior year of high school. Everything seemed to be going right. He had brought his grades up to a B+ average as a college football scout had urged him to. His scores on the college admission tests were even higher than he expected. All he needed was a strong football season his senior year. A full scholarship to the college of his choice was a sure thing.

Peter began a serious training program that spring. He did not want to risk being out of condition. He knew that the first day of football practice was in late August and he wanted to be ready for it. His training program was hard. He worked out at the gym every day, lifting weights to build his strength and muscle bulk. Every day he ran five miles to build up his endurance. He ate huge amounts of good food.

Peter refused to eat any foods that contained chemicals. He did not drink carbonated drinks. He limited the amount of fat and junk food he ate. He knew he had to be healthy and strong to play football.

Peter had always exercised. He was already enormous, compared to most kids in his class. He was tall and strong with big muscles on his arms and legs. Even his neck was too big for regular size shirts. The training program was certain to increase his strength and size even more. But Peter was worried. He knew scholarships were hard to get even with good grades. He wanted to bulk up even more; he wanted to get bigger fast.

He went to a health food store and found a book on nutritional supplements for athletes. The book was about vitamins, minerals, and things called amino acids. The book said amino acids could build muscle. He asked his parents about nutritional supplements; and his parents talked to Peter's doctor. The doctor told Peter to continue to eat healthy foods. He said Peter did not need nutritional supplements.

Peter did not usually ignore his parents' and doctor's advice. But he thought no one understood just how important the scholarship was. Peter went to the drugstore and bought many kinds of nutritional supplements. He began swallowing pills four times a day. He hated to swallow them, but he was determined to get bigger. He was not sure he noticed a difference, but he kept working hard.

By the end of June, Peter was stronger than he had ever been. He did not know if it was his hard work or the pills, but he did not care. There was hardly any fat on his body. He was all muscle. He was lifting heavier weights than he had ever lifted before. His speed was faster, and he did not get tired as quickly. He felt terrific. His friends noticed how good he looked. He had a new girlfriend who loved his strong muscles. But he was still worried that he was not big enough.

Some guys at the gym began telling Peter about drugs called anabolic steroids. The guys called these steroids "Magic Pills." They told Peter that steroids could bulk up even the weakest kid. They encouraged him to try them.

Peter had read a little about steroids. He had heard they were dangerous. He knew that he would not want to take them for long. He thought he might take low doses for a little while.

Peter felt that with steroids he might have a better chance for a winning season and the scholarship. He was sure he would not have any problems from the drug. After all, he figured, he had not had any problems with his nutritional supplements.

He hoped that maybe the steroids were nothing more than a different kind of nutritional supplement.

Peter found someone who would sell him a six-week supply of a drug called Anadrol for $175. The guy who had the pills said he could get in trouble if anyone found out and told Peter not to tell anyone about the pills. Peter decided to buy them. To get the money, he lied to his parents about why he needed so much cash. Once he had the pills, he felt a little strange taking medicine without his parents' permission. Still, he started taking them.

The change in Peter's body shortly after he began the steroids was dramatic. Without changing his eating or exercising routine, he put on 15 pounds in a matter of weeks. He was lifting heavier weights, having longer workout sessions, and running faster than ever. He was so impressed with what the one drug had done, he decided to experiment a little more. He wanted to be bigger.

He had a hard time explaining about the need for extra money to his parents, but they trusted him. He went back to his supplier and bought two new steroids. He began to do what the guys at the gym called stacking steroids. Stacking meant taking more than one pill at a time in higher doses than before. He knew higher doses were even more dangerous, but he felt the scholarship would be his payoff for taking the risk. Still he hated to lie to his parents about the money and the drugs.

Again, Peter had impressive gains. He could barely fit into any of his clothes because his muscles were so huge. But he also started to notice that he was developing pimples on his face.

Peter had never had acne before. He went to his doctor who asked him if he were taking any medicines. Peter was afraid to tell the truth, so he said he was only taking nutritional supplements. The doctor gave him some cream for his acne and told him to stop taking the supplements.

Peter continued to take the steroids. The acne on his face became worse. He had heard that steroids caused bad pimples. He just kept thinking of the scholarship and tried not to look in the mirror.

Peter also noticed that his mood was changing. Little things could throw him into a rage. One day he was having a small disagreement with his girlfriend. Before he knew it, he picked her up and threw her across the room. She landed on the couch and hurt her neck. Her parents came running into the room and made him leave. They told him he could never date their daughter again. He felt awful and tried to apologize.

Such outrage was just not like him, Peter thought. He had always been such an easygoing guy. He had heard that steroid use could make a person aggressive. He was sad to lose his girlfriend, but decided that he would have broken up with her to go to college anyway. The nasty behavior from the steroids might give him an even better chance in football.

Football season was in full force now. He was this year's star. By the end of the season, it was clear that his scholarship was a sure thing. He was relieved, because now he felt he could stop taking steroids. He stopped taking them the day he received the letter telling him he had won the full scholarship.

A few days later, Peter became very ill. He was sick to his stomach and could not keep any foods down. He realized he was going through drug withdrawal, but kept reminding himself that his scholarship had made it all worthwhile.

Peter made it through the winter without taking any steroids. He noticed that his face completely cleared up. He also noticed that he did not get angry as easily.

He felt even more sorry for the way he had treated his girl-friend. She would not even talk to him anymore. He wanted to tell her he behaved badly because of the steroids.

Peter noticed other changes since he had stopped the steroids. Although he had continued to train, his body was losing most of the muscle bulk and strength he had gotten while on the steroids. He was much smaller and weaker, he thought. By spring when he began his workouts for the fall college football season, he could not rebuild the muscle bulk he had lost.

Sadly, he believed that if he wanted to keep his scholarship, he would have to resume his use of steroids. He put off starting them until after the Senior Prom, however. He was afraid of the terrible acne he was sure to get. But by waiting so long he did not have as much time to bulk up. He talked to a few guys at the gym and they told him about a stronger drug. It was a pure male hormone, Testosterone. The only problem was that he had to inject the drug into his body with a needle. He hated shots.

Peter was afraid at first, but he was as determined as ever to keep his scholarship. He started giving himself daily shots. Again, in an even shorter time, he gained amazing size and strength. But by summer his face, back, and chest broke out in a bad case of acne. His once-smooth skin was becoming pitted from all the pimples.

Again his mood became nasty. Little things set him off in a rage. But something even worse happened. One day while he was lifting weights, his right shoulder joint popped. It felt loose. His arm hung and he couldn't move it. He was in great pain.

His parents brought him to his doctor. The doctor told Peter his shoulder joint had been badly torn by the weight of his own muscles.

The doctor explained that the only way a person could build such huge muscles was by taking steroids. The doctor asked him directly if he was taking anabolic steroids.

Peter had lied to the doctor before about his pimples. This time he was too scared and in too much pain to lie.

Peter admitted that he was taking daily shots of Testosterone and that he had taken other steroids. His mother started crying. His father shook his head and left the room.

The doctor told him his shoulder was badly damaged. He would need surgery to repair it. The doctor also told Peter that even with the operation it was doubtful he would ever be able to play football again. Peter tried to explain about the scholarship. He would lose it if he did not play football. The doctor said there was nothing he could do. Everything that had happened could have been prevented if Peter had not taken steroids.

Peter lost his scholarship. After the operation, he had limited movement in his shoulder. It would be like that for the rest of his life. Peter began reading about steroids. He learned some scary facts about his experimentation. He found out that steroids can cause liver cancer, kidney disease, and heart disease. He also learned that use of steroids can cause men to lose the ability to have children.

But the most frightening thing Peter learned was that even after someone stopped taking steroids, the bad effects could develop slowly over time. The lost scholarship and torn shoulder were the least of Peter's worries. Now he had to live each day knowing that the choice he had made could one day threaten his life.

3

CHOICES AND CONSEQUENCES

A choice is the act of selecting one thing or behavior over another. A consequence is the outcome or result of the choice made. Every choice has a consequence. Some choices are good, and some consequences are good. Other choices are poor, and the consequences are bad.

Peter made many choices as he tried to win a college football scholarship. First he worked to earn the kind of grades that the college said he would need. Next, he worked to be as strong as possible. He ate only healthy foods—no chemicals, junk food, and little fat. He chose to exercise every day. Although he looked and felt good, he decided he needed something more.

Peter chose first to read about vitamins, minerals, and amino acids and discuss them with his parents and doctor. Despite their discouragement, he chose to try them.

From there he chose to experiment with steroids. He chose to lie to his parents to get the money. Even though the risks of taking steroids were great, he chose to ignore them. He chose to place the college scholarship above his parent's advice and trust. He put the scholarship above his friendship with his girlfriend. He also chose to place the scholarship above the steroids' early effects, such as bad acne and temper outbursts.

Peter's choices are shown in the chart below with the good and bad outcomes.

PETER'S CHOICES	CONSEQUENCES	
	GOOD OUTCOMES	*BAD OUTCOMES*
1. Earn good grades.	Win scholarship Get respect of teachers. Make parents proud. Have self-respect and pride.	Hard work.
2. Eat healthy foods and exercise.	Maintain health Feel good. Look good. Have self-respect and pride.	Takes time and self-discipline.

3. Read about nutritional supplements and discuss with parents and doctor.	Become fully informed. Learn to think critically. Behave intelligently. Have self-respect.	Takes time.
4. Take nutritional supplements.		Go against parents' and doctor's advice. Risk illness if taken wrong. Develop false sense of well being. Waste money. Lose self-respect for being dishonest.
5. Take steroids.	Gain muscle strength and size.	Risk getting in trouble with school and parents and losing their respect. Risk losing self-respect. Risk scholarship and college.

CONSEQUENCES

GOOD OUTCOMES	*BAD OUTCOMES*
	Risk health and behavior problems. Risk future health problems. Betray own sense of right and wrong.

   In the first three choices, the benefits of the good outcomes outnumbered the risks of the bad. Peter behaved in a thoughtful, intelligent way. He thought critically by considering the good and the bad outcomes. He made good choices.

   In the last two choices, the risks of the bad outcomes outnumbered the benefits of the good. Peter, although very bright, may not have considered all the risks to his choices. In some cases, he acted impulsively, without thought. He may have given up his own sense of right and wrong. Perhaps he became too focused on a scholarship. He excused his actions and choices based on his goal of getting a scholarship. The end result was more important than what he had to do to get there.

   In choices four and five, Peter abandoned his code of values. He gave up his sense of right and wrong. He lost his own standards of who he was. While he would not eat foods with chemicals, he took large amounts of dangerous chemicals in the form of pills and shots. He not only risked his health, he also risked his own identity and values.

By failing to consider all the possible consequences of taking steroids, Peter destroyed, rather than improved, his chances for the scholarship. The worst outcome, however, is that a more serious disease may develop as Peter gets older.

This 13-year-old boy has learned that crimes have consequences.

4

DRUG FACTS AND STATISTICS

Drugs are chemical substances that affect the body. The use of illegal chemical substances by children and teenagers occurs in all cultures regardless of income or race. In the 1990s, hundreds of drugs are available to young people.

Usually, people do not use dangerous drugs right away. In studying drug use among children and teens, experts have found that most people follow a pattern of substance abuse. This pattern has four stages.

Stage one is experimentation; a person tries a drug. Some people call this the use stage because the person is using the drug once in awhile. Pressure from friends to use the drug may be the reason for first-time drug use. If the drug seems to give the person what they want from it, they may continue to experiment with that same drug mostly at parties and with friends.

The most common first drug used by young people is tobacco. The second is alcohol. The third is marijuana. The younger a person is when drugs are first tried, the more likely they are to develop more serious problems later on. Children under 15 years of age are at the most risk. Some kids believe that using tobacco is safe. They believe that they are in control. However, 90 percent of casual cigarette smokers develop into addicted smokers. So even the experimental stage can be dangerous.

A person enters stage two when they regularly use a drug. Some people call this the abuse stage because the person is overusing the drug.

At this stage, the person may be using the drug daily and not just at parties. The person may use the drug when they are alone, on school days, or early in the morning. They know how the drug is supposed to feel and work.

All drugs enter a person's blood and can affect the entire body. Because the drug goes into the blood, it can cause both desired and undesired body responses. Undesired body responses are called side effects.

Tobacco is most often the first drug that young people try. Tobacco use is common among young people in many cultures. These boys are from Bosnia.

Examples of side effects may be coughing from cigarettes, acne from steroids, headaches from alcohol, or memory loss from marijuana.

In stage two, people learn to accept the unpleasant side effects of the drug. Their goal is to keep a supply of the drug, because they like to experience what they see as the benefit of the drug. In the case of alcohol, tobacco, and marijuana, young people may want to use the drug because it makes them feel older, more relaxed, or takes away pain. In the case of steroids, the muscle growth is the desired effect.

In this stage, people may experiment with new drugs. They are usually dishonest with parents, other family members, and some friends. They may do poorly in school. They may pull away from old friends and family to spend more time with their friends who use drugs.

In stage three, a person needs a drug to get along with everyday life. Some people call this the dependent stage because the person depends on the drug to feel normal. The body craves the drug and needs it to function. Without the drug, they may get very sick and experience withdrawal from the drug.

Some kids at this stage also depend on the drug for emotional support. This means they are addicted to the drug. They may try to stop taking the substance, but find they cannot stay away from it. They spend a lot of time trying to figure out how to keep their drug supply full, because they need a lot of money to buy the drug. Some kids at this stage will do something illegal to get drugs. They may sell drugs to make enough money to buy drugs for themselves. They may steal things and sell them for money.

They spend a lot of time alone. Most of their life centers around getting the drug they need.

Stage four is the final stage when the mind and body begin to break down from drug abuse. The person becomes sick. Some people call this the burnout stage because the mind and body have been badly

*Marijuana is usually the third drug most young people try.
Alcohol is second. The photo above is of marijuana cigarettes
and a pipe, which is often used in smoking the drug.*

damaged by the side effects of the substance. At stage four, if the drug is not stopped, the person will likely die from the bad side effects.

Hundreds of drugs are used by young people around the world. The most common drugs used by children in the United States in the 1990s are: tobacco; alcohol; marijuana; cocaine; inhaled substances, such as glue; stimulants (drugs that wake a person up); tranquilizers (drugs that calm a person down); hallucinogens (drugs that make a person see or hear things that are not there); PCP; heroin; diet pills; anabolic steroids; and prescription drugs (taken by someone without a doctor's order).

Some children are more at risk to use and abuse drugs than others. Children with family members who were alcoholics or drug addicts are at the greatest risk of developing problems with substances. Even small amounts of experimenting with a drug may cause these children to become addicted.

Families may place children at higher risk of having a drug problem. For example, children are more likely to try substances if their parents smoke, drink, or use drugs. These young people may also try drugs if their parents have not told them that substances are bad. Children whose parents hurt or abuse them are at more risk of trying drugs. Children with parents who do not provide rules or who leave their children alone are at greater risk of trying drugs.

Good family relationships with fair rules and discipline give children some protection from trying drugs in the first place. The better they feel about themselves, the less likely they will choose drugs.

Children with friends or brothers and sisters who use chemicals are more likely to try drugs than kids who are not around drug-using friends. Children who move a lot and change schools seem to be at more risk. Children who attend parties where drugs are available are more likely to use them. Children in a stable home with loving parents are less likely to use drugs.

Each person is different. A person's own values and attitudes can affect whether they are at risk of trying drugs. Children who are aware of the medical and legal consequences of drug abuse are at a lower risk of drug use. Children who fail in school are at greater risk of trying drugs. The more a student uses drugs, the less likely they will finish school. The more a student knows about drugs, the less likely they will try them.

People on drugs often do not have good judgment and self-control. The drugs impair their thinking. In the United States, use of tobacco, alcohol, and other drugs causes motor vehicle crashes, murders, suicides, and cancer.

Accidents are the leading cause of death among teenagers. Of the 25,000 accidental deaths among young people each year, 10,000 are alcohol related. Drug use is a leading cause of death among teenagers.

Drug use also causes an increase in teenage pregnancy and sexually transmitted diseases. This is because people on drugs often make poor choices. It is thought that about 11 percent of all pregnant women use drugs. As a result, about 10 million children in the United States are raised by addicted parents. Babies can be born addicted to drugs if their mother took drugs during the pregnancy. These babies can also be born with brain and body damage.

The United States has the highest rate of drug abuse of all countries. In 1992, experts compared Amsterdam, Netherlands, and Washington, D.C. There were 40 murders in Amsterdam, Netherlands. Fifteen of them were drug related. In that same year, there were 480 murders in Washington, D.C. Of those murders, 240 were drug related.

Drug use is a major cause of teenage pregnancy.

In 1991, the United States Centers for Disease Control reported statistics on drug use in American youths in grades 9 through 12. Their findings are below:

SUBSTANCE PERCENT REPORTING USE

	AT LEAST ONCE IN THE PAST MONTH	*EVER IN THEIR LIFE*
cigarettes	32	82
smokeless tobacco	10	N/A
any alcohol	59	88
5 or more drinks at one time	37	43
marijuana	14	31
cocaine	2	7
steroids	N/A	5

Following are other startling facts about drug use and young people:

- More than 90 percent of U.S. high school seniors will have used alcohol before high school graduation.
- 50 percent of seniors will have used marijuana before graduation.
- 22 percent of young people who used drugs tried their first alcohol in seventh or eighth grade, according to a 1986 U.S. Department of Health study.
- 11 percent of young people tried marijuana for the first time in those same grades.
- The number of males using drugs is more than the number of females using drugs. However, a large increase in the number of

- In 1988, the National Institute on Drug Abuse (NIDA) estimated that 30 million Americans had tried cocaine. In that same
year, 57 million Americans used cigarettes; 106 million Ameri
cans used alcohol.
- In November 1993, the Center on Addiction and Substance
Abuse at Columbia University estimated substance abuse
causes 500,000 deaths a year. It drains $250 billion from the
U.S. health care system. Most of this is due to legal drugs:
alcohol and tobacco.

5

THE CASE FOR LEGALIZING DRUGS

Some experts believe that the war on drugs is hopeless. They also believe that drug addiction is an illness or disease, not a crime. Because of their beliefs, they think that drugs should be legalized. They believe that legalizing drugs will allow addicted people to seek help for their illness without fear of punishment. If legalized drugs were controlled, diseases related to street drugs would also be controlled.

Michael Gazzaniga, a scientist at Dartmouth Medical School, believes that every society has a natural level of drug abuse. He feels that as one substance is on the increase, another decreases. The overall number of people who use drugs, he said, will remain the same, whether drugs are legal or illegal.

U.S. Surgeon General Jocelyn Elders has suggested that drug legalization needs serious examination. Her reason is that drug addiction is a disease. Her goal is to help treat addicts and educate young people to never try drugs in the first place.

To do this takes money. By legalizing drugs, money now spent to hunt down drug users could be spent to help them.

President Bill Clinton's stepfather was an alcoholic and his brother was addicted to drugs. In February 1994, Clinton announced a new antidrug policy. He increased treatment and prevention money by $1 billion. He increased the amount of money, but not by as much, to stopping the illegal sale of drugs. His drug budget shows he wants to treat addiction like a disease more than a crime.

President Bill Clinton announced a new antidrug policy in 1994 that will combat addiction.

In February 1994, Robert Reno of *Newsday* magazine wrote that the greatest threat of drugs to the public is not from the drugs. He believes the problem is from the violent crimes associated with drug-seeking behavior. If drugs like marijuana and cocaine were treated like tobacco and alcohol, Reno believes billions of dollars now spent on criminal drug enforcement would be saved. This money could be spent on drug education and treatment.

Reno pointed out that alcohol use remained about the same both before and after Prohibition. (The passage of a Prohibition law in 1919 made it illegal to make or sell alcoholic beverages. The law was repealed in 1933.) He explained that if drugs were legalized, drug use would stay the same. He wonders if people who used drugs before they were legal would also use them after they were legal. He said this would be especially true if the government put its effort into education to prevent people from trying drugs in the first place.

In February 1990, the Drug Policy Foundation, an agency that supports drug legalization, released a poll. It said 36 percent of Americans favor some form of legalization.

Clare Regan, editor of a newsletter for a citizens' action group that focuses on crime, believes drugs should be legalized. She points out that in countries that have changed their laws, improvements have been made. She explained that Germany, the Netherlands, Switzerland, England, and Australia have some controls on drug possession and sales. Regan believes these countries have reduced crime by drug users. She also thinks these countries have fewer cases of drug-related diseases than the United States.

Finally, she feels these countries have more people in drug treatment programs. Legalization in the United States, she believes, would result in safer drugs and less violence.

6

THE CASE AGAINST LEGALIZING DRUGS

In 1991, Michael Parenti of *Political Affairs* magazine wrote that when something is made legal, it becomes more available. The more available it is, the more people use it. He pointed out that there are already two legalized drugs: alcohol and tobacco.

Alcohol kills 30 times more people than other abused drugs. Tobacco kills 60 times more people than other abused drugs. Parenti believes that if other abused drugs were legalized, deaths from these substances would rise. He disagrees that alcohol use was the same both before and after Prohibition. He stated that after it was made legal, alcohol use increased and so did alcohol-related disease.

In 1990, Senator Charles B. Rangel, chairman of the House Select Committee on Narcotics, wrote an article in *USA Today*.

He expressed concern that if drugs were legalized, the wrong message would be sent to kids. The message would be that drugs are safe. He disagreed with Clare Regan's findings. He said that legalized drugs did not improve the situation in the Netherlands. He pointed out that in 1983, after heroin had been legalized, Amsterdam had more drug-related murders than any other city in the world.

Gabriel Nahas, a pharmacologist at Columbia University's College of Physicians, warned against legalizing drugs. He said throughout history available drugs have been damaging. In societies where addictive drugs are socially accepted, he states there has been great damage to the people and the society. He also believes that legalization of heroin in Britain has been a failure.

Richard Millstein, acting director of NIDA, talked about why drug use by teenagers increased between 1992 and 1993. He felt attitudes by teens toward drugs are changing. He believes many young people now see drug use as a normal part of growing up. He felt much of this is because there is an attitude that drugs, alcohol, and tobacco are glamorous.

William Bennett, head of the drug policy office under President George Bush, stated that drug use among teenagers is on the rise because the government has loosened its policies against drugs. He disagrees with Surgeon General Jocelyn Elders that drugs should be legalized.

The NIDA survey of high school students showed that legal drugs (tobacco and alcohol) are the most widely used drugs at all grade levels. People against legalizing drugs believe this is proof that if other drugs are made legal, more kids will use them.

7

VALUES

A value is a quality held in high regard by a society. The story of Peter is about a teenager who experimented with dangerous drugs. It is also about values.

Peter had many meaningful values in life. College was important to him. He studied hard and earned good grades. He knew it was wise to learn about something before he tried it. He valued books and discussions with his parents and doctor. He made a bad choice, but at least he understood the importance of trying to make well-informed decisions. Perhaps if he had learned more about steroids before he tried them, he would not have used them.

Peter recognized the importance of taking care of his body with good food and regular exercise. A mistake he made was to think that nutritional supplements and steroids were a quicker way to get what he wanted. He still worked hard. He had good self-discipline.

Even when he used steroids a second time, Peter understood that he was wrong. He recognized the bad effects the drug was having on him.

Peter did not stop himself, though, because he felt he had no other way to win the scholarship. Perhaps a lesson he needed to learn was to believe in himself. He might have been able to win the scholarship without the drugs after all. Unfortunately, Peter will never know the answer to that question.

People make decisions based on their values. The decision to use or sell illegal drugs will affect a person's value structure.

8

YOUR TURN

You've read about a person using drugs and some facts about drug use and abuse. You've also read the basic arguments for and against the legalization of drugs. Now it's your turn to voice your opinion and start thinking of your own solutions. Below are some points to think about either alone or in a group. With each point, be creative in your problem solving.

1. Pretend you've been invited to a party and when you arrive, no grown-ups are around. Your friends are smoking and drinking and offer you a cigarette and a can of beer. You don't want to use drugs, but you also don't want your friends to make fun of you. Make a list of ten things you might say to refuse the drugs. Form a small group and act out the situation. Use your list and practice your different ways to say no.

2. Become aware of how drugs and alcohol are promoted. In a regular notebook or on a sheet of paper, keep a Drug Advertisement Journal for one week.

Every time you see or hear a message promoting beer or other alcoholic beverages, cigarettes, diet pills, and medicines, make a note of it. Watch for ads on TV, in song lyrics, on billboards, and in newspapers and magazines.

Advertisers often send hidden messages to make you believe that using their product will help you. Sometimes these messages are real and based on facts. Sometimes these messages are not real and based on myths. In your entry, include the hidden message of the ad.

At the end of the week, look at your list. Are you surprised by the number of entries? Do you feel that the ads persuade people to use drugs? Why or why not?

3. Divide a sheet of paper into two columns. Label the first column "Drug Myths." Label the other "Drug Realities." Use your journal entries from number two to find the messages advertisers try to promote. Read each entry. If the message is a myth, write it in the first column. Then write a more realistic statement about the drug being advertised.

For example, a beer commercial may show a muscular, healthy man in a bathing suit sharing a beer with a beautiful woman in a bikini. The hidden message may be, "If you drink beer, you will be healthy." How could you find out if this is a myth or fact? Look at the other messages from the ads. Determine if their messages are fact or myth.

4. The more you know about drugs, the less likely you are to use them. Select one drug that young people in the United States are using today. At the library, read all you can about it. Take notes to remember how the drug looks. Note the long- and short-term drug effects. Learn the consequences of using the drug. Find out what effects the drug has on different parts of the body. Think about other consequences the drug may have on a family, society, and the user.

Once you have all this information, make your own advertisement. Is this a drug you want to promote or discourage? Make a poster about the drug you studied. Display your poster in a central spot in your school.

5. In Peter's story, he used his goal of receiving a scholarship as an excuse for many choices he made. He wanted to win at all costs; his end (winning the scholarship) justified his means (using anabolic steroids). He acted as though everything he did was okay as long as he got what he wanted—and as long as he did not get caught.

Take time to look at your own life and the choices you've made. Once a day for the next five days sit quietly in a dim room by yourself for at least ten minutes. Close your eyes. Breathe slowly. Relax your body. Think about how you lived your life today. Did you live as if everything you did, said, or thought mattered? Did you live as if the end result was all that counted? Did it matter how you achieved a goal? Did you find yourself living up to your own values? Did you follow your own mind? Were you swayed by others? After you've sat quietly, write down those things you did today that you were proud of. Write down those things you did that you want to change. Compare each day to see if your choices are making you live your life as though everything you do matters.

GLOSSARY

Amino Acids: the building blocks of protein.

Anabolic steroid: a type of drug that, when taken in high doses, has the ability to build muscle tissue. These chemicals are man-made yet similar to some natural chemicals found in humans.

Dose: a drug amount.

Endurance: the ability to keep going; endurance improves with exercise.

Nutritional supplements: substances taken to provide nutrients to the body that a person may not get from eating a well-balanced diet. Vitamins, minerals, amino acids, and proteins are all nutritional supplements.

Sexually transmitted diseases (STDs): infections passed from one sexual partner to another.

Side effect: undesired effects of a drug on the body.

Stacking: using several anabolic steroids together in doses to build muscle tissue faster than is possible by exercise alone.

Testosterone: a powerful male hormone found naturally in the body that gives a man male features.

Withdrawal: the body's response to the lack of a drug the body has become dependent on to function normally; withdrawal usually makes a person feel ill and irritable; most drug withdrawal should be treated by a doctor.

Index

A

acne 10, 11, 14, 20
addict 19, 20, 22, 23, 26, 27, 30
alcohol 19, 20, 21, 22, 23, 24, 25, 27, 28, 29, 30, 33, 34
amino acids 8, 14
Amsterdam 23, 30
anabolic steroids 6, 8, 11, 21, 35
Australia 28

B

Bennett, William 30
body damage 23
burnout stage 20

C

Center on Addiction and Substance Abuse 25
Centers for Disease Control 24
chemicals 8, 13, 16, 22
choices 4, 6, 13, 14, 16, 23, 35
cigarette 19, 20, 24, 25, 33, 34
Clinton, Bill 27
cocaine 6, 21, 24, 25, 28
crack cocaine 6

D

decision 4, 31
dependent stage 20
Drug Policy Foundation 28
drug treatment 28

E

education 39
Elders, U.S. Surgeon General Jocelyn 26
England 28

experimentation 12, 18

G

Germany 28

H

hallucinogens 21
heart disease 12
heroin 21, 30
hormone 11
House Select Committee on Narcotics 29

I

inhaled substances 21

J

junk food 8, 13

K

kidney disease 12

L

legalization of drugs 6, 33
liver cancer 12

M

marijuana 19, 20, 21, 24, 28
Parenti, Michael 29
minerals 8, 14
murder 22, 23, 30

N

National Institute on Drug Abuse (NIDA) 25
Netherlands 23, 28, 30
New York 39
NIDA 25, 30

nutritional supplements 8, 9, 10, 32

P

PCP 21
pills 8, 9, 16, 21, 34
prescription drugs 21
Prohibition 28, 29

R

Reno, Robert 28

S

Rangel, Senator Charles B. 29
side effects 19, 20, 21
stacking 9
statistics 6, 24
steroids 8, 9, 10, 11, 12, 14, 15, 16, 20, 21, 22, 31, 32, 35
stimulants 21
suicide 22

T

teenage pregnancy 23
television 4
testosterone 11, 12
tobacco 19, 20, 21, 22, 24, 25, 28, 29, 30
tranquilizers 21

V

value 6, 16, 22, 31, 35
vehicle crashes 22
vitamins 8, 14

W

Washington, D.C. 23
withdrawal 10, 20

For Further Reading

•*Growing up Drug Free: A Parents Guide to Prevention.* U.S Department of Education Publication. Available free of charge by writing

National Clearinghouse for Alcohol & Drug Information
P.O. Box 2345
Rockville, MD 20852

ABOUT THE AUTHOR

Dr. Cynthia DiLaura Devore, a pediatrician specializing in school health, is a former special educator and speech pathologist. Her role as a school physician blends her training and experience in both education and medicine. She is the author of a series of books for children covering issues of loss and separation. That series, Children of Courage, is available through Abdo & Daughters. Dr. Devore lives in Rochester, New York, with her husband and two sons.